Compliments of W. F.

[*From the Sixth Annual Report of the Mass. State Board of Health.*]

VENTILATION OF RAILROAD CARS,

BY THEO. W. FISHER, M.D.

OF BOSTON.

WITH CHEMICAL ANALYSES,

BY WM. RIPLEY NICHOLS,

PROFESSOR OF GENERAL CHEMISTRY IN THE MASSACHUSETTS INSTITUTE OF TECHNOLOGY.

BOSTON:

WRIGHT & POTTER, STATE PRINTERS,

79 MILK STREET (CORNER OF FEDERAL).

1875.

VENTILATION OF RAILROAD CARS.

By THEO. W. FISHER, M. D.
(Of Boston.)

WITH CHEMICAL ANALYSES,

By WM. RIPLEY NICHOLS,
Professor of General Chemistry in the Massachusetts Institute of Technology.

VENTILATION OF RAILROAD CARS.

The object of this paper is briefly to call public attention to the insanitary condition of the passenger-cars on our railroads, and to introduce some tests and experiments on the air in smoking and other cars made by Prof. W. R. Nichols, of the Massachusetts Institute of Technology, at the request of the State Board of Health.

This subject of car-ventilation may seem trivial when we consider the brief period of occupancy in individual cases, but even in this point of view, it is of some importance; and to that quite large class of persons who spend several hours daily in the cars, it is of the most vital interest. The American people are eminently a travelling public, and the aggregate of time spent in this way is worth considering. Massachusetts, according to the Railroad Commissioners' Report for 1873, has 1,735 miles of railroad, or about one mile to every 879 inhabitants, and to every four square miles of territory. The number of passengers carried annually is over forty-two millions. These facts show the importance of making all public conveyances equal, at least, in their hygienic condition, to our school-houses and other public buildings.

That this is not the case, the travelling public has daily sensible demonstration. Universally defective methods of heating and ventilation of steam-cars lead to bad air, oppressed breathing, hot, heavy and aching heads, cold feet, coughs and debility, to say nothing of the discomforts of heat, dust and bad odors in summer. To these are added the deleterious effects of the concentrated fumes of tobacco, when the traveller is driven for a seat to the smoking-car.

A striking illustration of how bad the condition of things

may become, is found in a monograph, by the Baron N. de Derschau,* a Russian engineer, upon Heating and Ventilation of Railway Cars (Paris, 1871). An experiment was made on an American car, running as third-class between St. Petersburg and Moscow, during the winter of 1866. The car was 50 feet long, and carried 80 passengers. The outside temperature at starting was 22° F. below zero, the inside 16° below, and there was no means of heating. Observations were made hourly, with the following result: The temperature rose from the accumulation of animal heat until, at the end of nine hours, it was, in the upper part of the car, 21° above zero, while on the floor it was still 6° below. The carbonic acid increased to alarming proportions; viz., from .140 per cent. at starting to .940 per cent. the last hour! The hygrometer, as well as the frost on the windows and the fog in the air, showed that the saturation point for moisture had been reached. The experimenter left the car at the ninth hour physically unable to continue his tests.

This was, of course, an extreme example of what exists in a less degree in every ill-ventilated car. In cold and rainy, or in hot and dusty weather, the opening of windows is impracticable, and passengers suffer the insidious effects of bad air in avoiding the more obvious dangers from dust and draughts. The opening of doors at stations affords but little relief, since the cars are not then in motion so as to create a thorough draught.

The smoking-car is a purely American institution. In England and France, smoking is forbidden in the first and second class carriages, but is connived at by the guards, on the payment of a small fee, if no one in the compartment objects. In Germany, smoking is so universal that a contrary custom prevails, and smoking is allowed everywhere, except in certain compartments marked "*Für nicht Raucher*" (no smoking), where tourists and ladies may avoid the fumes of pipe and cigar, if they wish. Our custom is to collect all smokers into one car, thus concentrating the products of burning tobacco, which might otherwise be diffused through the whole train.

The bad hygienic condition of these moving fumatories must be more or less familiar to all. The fact that the air is irrespirable by most non-smokers, including the whole female sex, is sufficient to show this without the aid of chemical tests, which often fail to detect subtle atmospheric qualities, which may be evident to the senses, and fruitful sources of disease and death. Exceptional mischief of a serious kind has recently served to direct attention to the above fact; a young man having been killed by falling from the platform of a moving train, in consequence, it was supposed, of the dizziness produced by a brief stay in the smoking-car.

The following experiments of Prof. Nichols will furnish approximate evidence of the purity of the air in cars, under various circumstances, by showing the amount of carbonic acid present. This gas is irrespirable, except in the smallest quantities, and is generally accepted as a fair standard of the amount of other impurities given off by the skin and lungs, which tend by their immediate putrefaction to produce directly poisonous effects upon the human system.

MASSACHUSETTS INSTITUTE OF TECHNOLOGY,
Boston, December 12, 1874.

DEAR SIR:—Having been requested by Dr. Folsom, Secretary of the State Board of Health, to make some investigations into the character of the air in smoking-cars, I beg leave to report herewith the results of such determinations as have been made.

Every one recognizes the "closeness" of the air on entering, at this season of the year, an ordinary passenger-car which is moderately full. We are not able to determine exactly the substances in the air which cause this feeling and which produce the injurious effects experienced by remaining for a considerable length of time in ill-ventilated or overcrowded apartments. As, however, the exhalations and emanations causing the injurious effects are always composed in part of, or attended by, *carbonic acid*, and as the amount of this compound can be estimated with great exactness, it is usual to take the carbonic acid as affording an indication of the completeness or deficiency of the ventilation.

In the case of smoking-cars, in addition to the exhalations and emanations from the passengers, the products of the tobacco consumed mix with the air and render it oppressive to most non-smokers. The products of the combustion of tobacco, if the combustion were complete, would be carbonic acid, ammonia and water; in the process of smoking, however, most of the tobacco is distilled rather than burned, and the products of this distillation are quite numerous and complex. The most complete investigation into the composition of tobacco-smoke with which I am acquainted, was made by Vohl and Eulenburg.* They smoked artificially a considerable quantity of tobacco and claim to have recognized with distinctness in the smoke, cyanhydric acid, sulphuretted hydrogen; certain acids of the fatty acid series,—namely, formic, acetic, propionic, butyric and valerianic; also, carbolic acid and creasote; also, pyridin, picolin, collidin and other similar alkaloïds, but no nicotin. They found also, in the smoke, ammonia, nitrogen and oxygen, and small quantities of marsh-gas and carbonic oxide.

I have made several attempts to obtain evidence, by chemical means, of the presence in the air of smoking-cars of some of the characteristic products of the smoking of tobacco, but without success, On one occasion I rode from Worcester to Boston, drawing a portion of the air of the car through proper absorbing media. The train was express, and the car was completely filled, and the smokers were about in the usual proportion,—perhaps one-half of the passengers were smoking. Of the peculiar components of the tobacco-smoke, it seemed to me that the fatty acids, so called, butyric, valerianic and acetic acids, would be bodies to be tested for with the greatest hope of success, but I tested also for the alkaloid bodies, which probably form the most injurious portions of the smoke. On this occasion 10 liters ($2\frac{1}{5}$ gallons) of air were drawn through the absorbing liquid, but the results were negative. On another occasion 30 liters of air were employed, and on several other occasions quantities lying between these two; in no case was I successful in separating and identifying any of these peculiar products. This, however, is not a matter of great surprise. Vohl and Eulenburg, in the experiments mentioned above, appear to have determined the character of the acid products by consuming 50 cigars, and the alkaline products by the consumption of 100

* Archiv der Pharmacie, [2] 147 (1871,) p. 130.

more. The statement is not, however, quite clear,* and the *amount* of any substance obtained is not given. The whole of the products of the distillation (except the permanent gases) were condensed by them or absorbed in appropriate liquids; in the actual process of smoking, a considerable quantity of these substances are absorbed by the smoker, and what does escape into the air is so diffused, even in a poorly ventilated car, that it would be necessary to use a very large amount of air in order to discover the peculiar bodies of tobacco-smoke, and even then the amount, except by the use of cars-full of air, would be too small to estimate quantitatively. A very little tobacco-smoke does indeed affect the eyes and throat of a person unaccustomed to its use, but our senses are often affected by quantities too small to weigh, too small even to detect by chemical means.

The question, then, from a chemical point of view, seemed to resolve itself into a question of ventilation, and a number of experiments were made to determine the amount of carbonic acid in the air of the cars. The results of these experiments are embodied in the following table.

The following experiments were made to see whether there was an increase of carbonic acid during the trip:—

* The process of separating the alkaloids required several fractional distillations and recrystallizations of the platinum compounds into which they were converted. The authors detail the separation, the identification by physical properties, the determination of the boiling-point, the elementary analysis, and the analysis of the platinum compounds in each case. It seems hardly possible that so small an amount of tobacco as indicated above, could have furnished the material for reliable determinations, and it is possible that some error may have crept into the statement of the amount.

TABLE NO. 1.—*Smoking-Cars.*

No.	Date.	Carbonic Acid in volumes, per cent.	RAILROAD.	Description of Train.	Sample taken between—
1	Nov. 4, .	0.233	Providence, .	Dedham train reaching Boston at 7.35 A. M., .	Roxbury and Boston.
2	4, .	0.261	" .		" "
3	4, .	0.173	" .	Same train as Nos. 1 and 2; different car, not so full, .	" "
4	7, .	0.335	" .	Dedham train reaching Boston at 7.18 A. M., .	" "
5	13, .	0.283	" .	Stoughton train reaching Boston at 8.10 A. M., .	" "
6	23, .	0.253	" .		" "
7	24, .	0 171	" .		" "
8	27, .	0.242	Fitchburg, .	Watertown Branch train leaving Boston at 5.55 P. M., .	Boston and Cambridge.
9	27, .	0.140	" .		Cambridge and Mt. Auburn.
10	Dec. 3, .	0.369	Providence, .	Dedham train, due in Boston at 7.35 A. M., .	Boylston and Boston.
11	3, .	0.317	" .	Stoughton train, due in Boston at 8.10 A. M., .	" "
12	4, .	0.098	Eastern, .	Train leaving Boston at 5 P. M., .	Boston and Lynn.
13	4, .	0.127	" .	Train reaching Boston at 6.25 P. M., .	Lynn and Boston.
14	9, .	0.234	Fitchburg, .	Same train as Nos. 8 and 9, .	Boston and Cambridge.
15	9, .	0.179	" .		Cambridge and Mt. Auburn.

NOTE.—The method employed for estimating the carbonic acid, was that known as Pettenkofer's, and the air was taken at the height of the heads of the seated passengers.

The following determinations were made in ordinary passenger-cars :—

TABLE No. 2.—*Passenger-Cars.*

No.	Date.	Carbonic Acid in volumes, per cent.	RAILROAD.	Description of Train.	Samples taken between—
16	Nov. 13,	0.367	Providence, .	Stoughton train reaching Boston at 8.10 A. M., . .	Jamaica Plain and Boston.
17	24,	0.298	" .		" " "
18	Dec. 3,	0.174	" .	Dedham train reaching Boston at 7.18 A. M., . . .	Boylston and Boston.
19	3,	0.174	" .	Stoughton train reaching Boston at 8.10 A. M., . .	" "
20	8,	0.159	" .	Dedham train reaching Boston at 7.35 A. M., samples	" "
21	8,	0.219	" .	taken in different cars, ...	

NOTE.—The trains mentioned in Tables No. 1 and No. 2, were all local, and the greatest distance passed over, before the sample was taken, was about fourteen miles.

The air in the smoking-car of the Stonington steamboat train, on the Boston and Providence Railroad, was examined at intervals during the journey from Boston to Providence, Friday, December 11, 1874. The train left Boston at 5.30 P.M., reaching Providence at 7.05 P.M. The capacity of the car was about 2,750 cubic feet net. The number of passengers was thirty-seven, of whom eighteen were smoking. This was about the average during the trip.

No.	Carbonic Acid volume, per cent.	TIME.	Length of Time.	After leaving—
1	0.172	5.35 P. M., ...	5 minutes,	Boston.
2	0.158	5.50 "	20 "	Boston.
3	0.153	6.05 "	35 "	Boston.
	–	6.10 "	*	–
4	0.194	6.15 "	5 "	Sharon.
	–	6.22 "	†	–
5	0.165	6.35 "	12 "	Mansfield.
	–	6.38 "	‡	–
6	0.177	6.45 "	7 "	Attleborough.

* Train stopped at Sharon. † Train stopped at Mansfield.
‡ Train stopped at Attleborough.

A somewhat similar experiment (but less extended) was made December 9, 1874, on the Watertown branch of the Fitchburg Railroad. The capacity of the car (after deducting the space actually occupied by the passengers) was about 2,350 cubic feet.

No.	Carbonic Acid volume, per cent.	Number of Passengers.	Number Smoking.	TIME.	Train—
	–	–	–	5.55 P. M.	Left Boston.
	–	–	–	5.58 "	Left Charlestown.
1	0.234	44	15	6.05 "	– –
	–	–	–	6.07 "	Stopped at Cambridge.
2	0.179	34	8	6.10 "	– –
	–	–	–	6.13 "	Stopped at Mt. Auburn.

On several occasions, I made comparative tests for the *ammonia* present in smoking-cars and passenger-cars. The amounts in the following table are *comparative*, simply.

1.			Outer air, Back Bay, average,	100
2.	Nov.	13.	Providence Railroad smoking-car,	575
3.	Dec.	4.	Eastern Railroad smoking-car,	310
4.	"	4.	" " " " after stopping at a station,	266
5.	"	11.	Providence Railroad steamboat train, taken at same time as carbonic acid (No. 3) of same date,	400
6.	"	11.	Ditto. Taken at same time as carbonic acid (No. 6) of same date,	340
7.	"	8.	Providence Railroad, common car,	135
8.	"	8.	" " another "	175

I may remark, that more of the samples have been taken on the Providence Railroad than on any other, simply because it was more convenient of access.

Yours very respectfully,

WM. RIPLEY NICHOLS.

DR. T. W. FISHER.

The first fact noticeable in Prof. Nichols' report is, that the amount of carbonic acid found in cars exceeds considerably the average for public buildings, and is, of course, largely in excess of what would be found in the dwellings of the better classes, or in the open air. In the Report of the State Board of Health, for 1871, an article, by the late Dr. Derby, on "Air, and some of its Impurities," gives the average per cent. for the outer air in this vicinity as .035, and for school-houses as about .140. The Music Hall is set down at .140 after a concert; Municipal Court-room, .120; Globe Theatre, .144; Waiting-room of Public Library, from .136 to .193, etc.

The average of Table No. 1 gives the percentage for smoking-cars at .228, the lowest example being .127, and the highest .369. The average of Table No. 2 gives for passenger-cars a percentage of .232; lowest, .174; highest, .367. The air on the Stonington steamboat-train smoking-car was exceptionally pure, the average being .170. The car was by no means full, and but half were smoking. The smoking-cars of the New York express trains, on the Boston & Albany Railroad, would, perhaps, furnish more marked results. These cars will accommodate 70 passengers, and, according to Mr. F. D. Adams, of that road, are usually filled with smokers, who play euchre from Boston to New York, in an atmosphere of dense smoke. The ordinary ventilators are of no use in clearing the car, and wickets in the ends are required to make any impression on it.

The tables show also a second fact; viz., that the additional amount of carbonic acid produced by the combustion of a few ounces of tobacco is hardly appreciable. Prof. Nichols estimates that if all the carbon of the tobacco were completely burned to carbonic acid, the carbonic acid formed might amount in weight, at a maximum, to one-quarter more than the amount of tobacco consumed. In actual practice, however, much of the carbon is not burned to carbonic acid, but some is given off in the state of carbonic oxide, and more, probably, in the form of compounds of carbon and hydrogen in matters of the nature of tar. The carbonic acid from this source would not indicate, however, any additional impurities from the lungs and skin, and it may be disregarded. A newspaper paragraph is authority for the statement, that Dr. Otto Krause, of Annaberg, Saxony, has found nine per cent. of carbonic oxide in tobacco-smoke; but this seems a large amount.

Let us examine, then, this question of ventilation in another way. The average capacity of a passenger-car is about 2,500 cubic feet of net air-space, excluding that occupied by passengers and furniture. A smoking-car, as arranged with tables, chairs and sofas will accommodate at least 50, and an ordinary car 75 passengers. This gives, in the first case 50, and in the last 33⅓ cubic feet of air-space to each passenger. The amount of air-space and of air per hour to insure proper ventilation has been variously estimated. Army regulations for hospitals and barracks require from 1,000 to 1,500 cubic feet of air, changed hourly, per soldier. The British Royal Commissioners, appointed in 1857, recommend 600 cubic feet of air-space, and 20 feet of air per minute and per man. Ten feet per minute is the lowest estimate suggested in any case. Take 15 feet per minute, then, as an average, and the air in smoking-cars should be changed thoroughly at least every four minutes, and in ordinary cars every three minutes, to insure proper ventilation. It is evident this is never accomplished.

It may be useful to insert here a table from a standard French work, by Gen. Morin, on "Heating and Ventilation" (Paris, 1874). I have reduced the metres to feet for convenience' sake.

Volume of air necessary to introduce and withdraw hourly for each person, to insure good ventilation.

		Cubic feet.
Hospitals,	Ordinary sickness,	2,100–2,450
	Surgical and lying-in,	3,500
	Epidemic,	5,250
Prisons,		1,750
Workshops,	Ordinary,	2,100
	Unhealthy,	3,500
Barracks,	By day,	1,050
	By night,	1,750
Theatres,		1,400
Public halls,		2,100
Lecture rooms,		1,050
Schools,	Infant,	420–525
	Adult,	875–1,050
Stables,		6,300

These figures, Gen. Morin states, are based on direct observation, and are not in the least exaggerated. The point at which all sensible odor from effete animal matter disappears is taken as the limit of satisfactory ventilation. This limit is not usually reached while more than .06 per cent. of carbonic acid remains.

Dr. R. Angus Smith says, in his "Air and Rain," a work of undoubted authority: "We cannot accept a lower standard of carbonic acid than .06 per cent.; and uniform diffusion being supposed, we cannot preserve our minimum standard of purity with a less delivery of fresh air than 3,000 cubic feet per head per hour!" This limit is also recommended by Pettenkofer. It will be seen how wide of any such standard is the condition of our steam-cars when each passenger has only from $33\frac{1}{3}$ to 50 feet of air-space; and air so seldom changed as to leave a percentage of from 0.2 to 0.3 volumes of carbonic acid!

The heating and ventilation of cars seem to be inseparable subjects. The monogram of the Baron de Dershau treats of the former in quite a thorough manner. He mentions only to condemn the various methods in use, such as foot-warmers of hot water or hot tiles, hot-water pipes, stoves of porcelain and iron, and iron stoves outside the cars, over which air is conducted to the interior. He concludes that steam alone is adapted to the purpose; and it is impossible not to agree with him, when we think of the dangerous and unmanageable fire-boxes so universally in use with us. Our stoves, besides overheating the air when approaching a red-heat, as is often the case, are subject to as great extremes of temperature as a bad case of chills and fever. The heat is also badly diffused in the car, and is of little or no aid to ventilation.

Steam-heating is in use on some American railroads, as well as in Russia, Belgium, Germany and Austria. The Baron de Dershau gives a complete description, with plans and specifications, of a system which he has introduced with success in Russia and elsewhere. It consists, briefly, of a special boiler for every eight cars, placed in a small compartment at the end of one of them, and tended from the platform. The steam is conveyed along the roofs in pipes encased in felt, and fed by vertical pipes into heating-tubes along the sides of the car-floor, the water of condensation being returned to the boiler by a pipe beneath the cars.

This system seems to have had no special relation to the ventilation of the compartments to which it was applied. This was provided for by an opening in the roof, allowing for a temperate climate 22 and for a cold climate 28 square centimeters of area for each passenger. Air was admitted by ventilators under the eaves, with openings arranged to catch the draught of the moving train. In a car fitted up for the emperor's summer use, air was admitted through wire screens in the floor, and carried up through hollow pillars containing a cooling mixture, being discharged through small ornamental openings in the capitals into the car.

Most American cars are now made with the Wagner monitor-roof, with patent pipes and apertures for the exit of foul and heated air, in great number and variety. These are not efficient, however, without provision for the admission of fresh supplies of air from below. Side and end ventilators have therefore been devised for this purpose, but are all open to certain objections. Those in the letter-line over the windows are too high up, and, as well as the wicket-sashes in the doors and end-windows, expose passengers to severe draughts, and, consequently, are seldom allowed to be open.

The eighth annual report of the Master Car-builders' Association, in convention at Cincinnati in June of last year, contains the report of a committee on heating and ventilation of much interest. The discussion on this report clearly shows the difficulties of the subject, and the various opinions and experiences of the representatives of different railroads, as well as a disposition to do something to improve the construction of cars, with respect to their sanitary arrangements. The report admits fully the importance of ventilation, and quotes at length Dr. Smith's experiments upon himself in the lead-chamber. It admits that a car has hardly sufficient air-space for *four*, instead of seventy-five persons; and that the solid and liquid impurities given off by a car-full of passengers, amounting, according to Prof. Huxley's estimate, to two pounds every twenty minutes, will no more go out of roof-ventilators without forcing, than fire-damp out of a mine.

The top and letter-line ventilators have proved entirely inadequate to effect the requisite change of air. The arrangements for admitting air at the end of the car, depending on the motion of the train, are most efficient, but most objectionable on account of the draught. To admit 2,400 feet per minute, at as slow a rate as five feet per second, there must be an opening as large as the whole end of the car; to make a greater velocity endurable, the air must be distributed through the car before reaching the passengers.

The system of Messrs. Sanborn & Gates, 15 West Street, Boston, was mentioned very favorably by the committee. This consists in a fan-wheel, carried by a pulley attached to one of the axles, which forces air into the car, through a strainer of wire-gauze, at the first side window. The air is conducted around the roof in a 6-inch pipe, perforated at proper intervals, and finds its exit through registers in the floor. This apparatus has been applied to a car on the Boston & Albany Railroad, and was tested by a company of gentlemen well known to the public, in May last. The report of a committee of observation will be found in the "Boston Post," May 6, 1874. When the car had been thoroughly filled with smoke, on admitting the air it was entirely cleared in about six minutes. It is intended to regulate the temperature and moisture by means of a heater and evaporator.

Mr. Adams, of the Boston & Albany Railroad, says the above apparatus works well, except on up-grades, where speed is too low for the best effect. It seems evident that some combination of steam-heating and forced ventilation must some time be found to solve the problem under consideration, unless railroad companies continue to be deterred by the expense incidental to its introduction. It was not intended to go into a critical examination of methods here. Such practical questions are for car-builders and railroad corporations to consider. The public should see that the efforts of these parties are not suspended through motives of false economy, or a lack of appreciation of the importance of perfect ventilation for all passenger-cars, both summer and winter, and in all weathers.

www.ingramcontent.com/pod-product-compliance
Lightning Source LLC
LaVergne TN
LVHW020638110826
845149LV00004B/1261

* 9 7 8 1 4 1 8 1 9 0 8 5 9 *